KT-570-162

WITHDRAWN

KT 0604 6718

THE FACTS ABOUT
Diabetes

Claire Llewellyn

Belitha Press

KINGSTON UPON THAMES
PUBLIC LIBRARIES

9/01

06042678

ALL	CLASS
TW	J613
CAT	REF
P Laqq	

First published in the UK in 2001 by
Belitha Press Limited
London House, Great Eastern Wharf
Parkgate Road, London SW11 4NQ

Copyright © Belitha Press Limited 2001
Text by Claire Llewellyn
Illustrations by Tom Connell

Editor: Russell McLean
Designer: Helen James
Picture researcher: Frances Vargo
Medical consultant: Jill Humphries, community children's nurse,
    Welwyn Garden City

All rights reserved. No part of this book may be reproduced or utilized
in any form or by any means, electronic or mechanical, including
photocopying, recording or by any information storage and retrieval
system, without permission in writing from the publisher, except by
a reviewer who may quote brief passages in a review.

Quotes on pages 11, 19, 23, 24 and 27
are taken from Diabetes UK publications.

ISBN 1 84138 314 7

Printed in China

British Library Cataloguing in Publication Data
for this book is available from the British Library.

10 9 8 7 6 5 4 3 2 1

Picture acknowledgements:
John Birdsall Photography: 20b. Corbis: Jenny Woodcock/Reflections
Photolibrary 25t. James Davis Photography: 12. Diabetes UK: 5t. Eye
Ubiquitous: Bob Battersby 5b; Peter Blake 26b; Bennett Dean cover bl,
21t, 22b; Mostyn 3r, 6b; Yiorgos Nikiteas 27t; Paul Seheult 13b, 16b;
Skjold 25b. Sally & Richard Greenhill: Sally Greenhill 17b, 26t, 28t.
Photofusion: B. Apicella 13t; Janis Austin cover background, 4b; Richard
Eaton 19b; Ute Klaphake 29b; Christa Stadtler 18t, 20t; Bob Watkins 9b.
Rex Features: Woman's Weekly 21b; Mark Lloyd 23b; John Moran 22t;
Today/Gooch/Levenson 23t; Zoom/D.P.P.I. 3b, 27b. Science Photo Library:
Scott Camazine/Sue Trainor 11l; CC Studio 8b, 18b; Mark Clarke cover br,
3c, 4t, 10t, 16t, 29t; Gable/Jerrican 24t; James Holmes/Celltech Ltd 28b;
St Bartholomew's Hospital 19t; Saturn Stills 11r, 14, 24b. Telegraph
Colour Library: Hugh Burden 1, 17t; Tipp Howell cover bc, 8t;
Antonia Reeve 9t; Paul Windsor 7. David Towersey: 15.

Contents

What is diabetes? 4

What happens inside? 6

Types of diabetes 8

Injecting insulin 10

Who gets diabetes? 12

Checking sugar levels 14

Highs and lows 16

The diabetes clinic 18

Food and drink 20

Sport and exercise 22

Diabetes at home 24

Diabetes at school 26

Questions people ask 28

Glossary and further information 30

Index 32

Words in **bold** are explained
in the glossary on page 30

What is diabetes?

Diabetes is a serious condition that affects the way the body uses sugar. Someone with diabetes has too much sugar in their blood. They need treatment for this all their life.

The signs of diabetes

You cannot tell from the outside if someone has diabetes, but you can tell from the things they have to do. Many people with diabetes need to give themselves injections.

You can't tell just by looking whether someone has diabetes.

Children with diabetes have to learn to give themselves injections.

The right amount of sugar

The injections give the body an important substance called **insulin** (see pages 6-7). This controls the amount of sugar in the blood. People with diabetes also need to think carefully about which foods they eat and when. This helps to make sure they get the right amount of sugar all through the day and night.

Damage to the body

People with diabetes can never forget their condition – it needs to be carefully controlled at all times. If it is not treated, diabetes causes tiredness and weight loss, and damages parts of the body such as the heart, **kidneys**, eyes and feet. This can be very dangerous.

Diabetes is a condition that affects both young and old.

Living with diabetes

Many people have to live with diabetes. This is how some of them describe what it is like:

'*I need to watch what I eat.*'

'*I have to inject myself every day.*'

'*I need to have snacks all the time.*'

'*I'm always doing blood tests.*'

'*I get tired and shaky sometimes.*'

People with diabetes need to think about which foods they eat and when.

What happens inside?

Our bodies use the sugar in blood as fuel. If a person has diabetes, their body is unable to use sugar because they are missing an important substance called insulin.

From food to fuel

When we eat, our food is broken down into different forms that the body can use. One group of foods, known as **carbohydrates**, are turned into a sugar called **glucose**, which quickly enters the **bloodstream**.

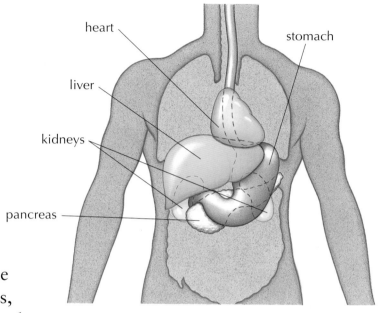

Insulin is made by special cells inside the pancreas. This is a long, thin gland behind the stomach.

As soon as the amount of sugar in the blood begins to rise, a **gland** called the **pancreas** begins to make insulin. Its job is to help the sugar enter the body's **cells**, which then use it as fuel. As we burn this fuel – by working, playing and just being alive – our sugar levels begin to fall. When this happens, the pancreas stops producing insulin until sugar levels in the blood rise again.

Pasta is one kind of carbohydrate.

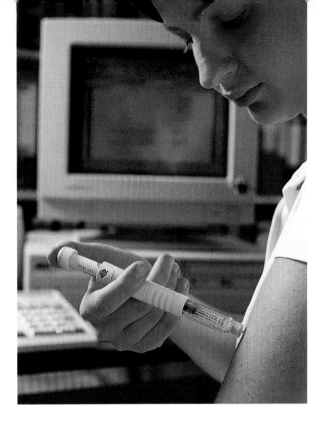

Insulin injections help people with diabetes to keep their blood sugar levels normal.

The trouble with diabetes

When someone has diabetes, glucose enters the bloodstream but cannot get into the body's cells. This is because the pancreas does not work properly and cannot produce insulin. So the sugar stays in the bloodstream. The level rises higher and higher. Eventually there is so much sugar in the blood that it overflows into the person's **urine**.

Did you know?

- Diabetes mellitus is the full name for diabetes. It comes from the Greek for 'fountain of honey'. This describes the sweet-smelling urine of someone with diabetes.
- People with diabetes may have a blood sugar level that is up to ten times higher than normal.
- Carbohydrates are divided into sugary foods, such as cakes and biscuits, and **starchy** foods such as bread, **chapati**, **plantain**, potatoes, pasta, cereals and rice.

What happens next?

When extra sugar leaks into their urine, a person needs to urinate, or wee, a lot. They need to drink lots of water to make up the lost fluids. More importantly, a person with diabetes does not make fuel from their food. They feel tired and start to lose weight.

Solving the problem

People with diabetes need to give their body the insulin it cannot make itself. They do this by giving themselves injections of insulin every day. Injected insulin does the same job as insulin made by the body – it helps glucose to enter the cells, and keeps sugar levels normal.

Types of diabetes

There are two types of diabetes. Children and young people usually have one type, while older people have the other. Both types of diabetes are caused by a lack of insulin, but are treated in different ways.

Type 1 diabetes

The kind of diabetes that most often affects children and young people is known as type 1. In type 1 diabetes, the pancreas cannot make insulin. Doctors do not know why this happens, but there are a number of possible reasons (see pages 12-13).

A strong thirst is an important early symptom of diabetes.

Type 1 diabetes develops very quickly, in some cases over just a few weeks. The **symptoms** can be severe, but fortunately the condition is easily **diagnosed**. There is no known cure for type 1, but it can be controlled quickly with injections of insulin, a healthy diet, and exercise.

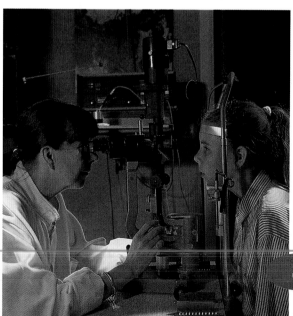

An optician may be the first person to notice that someone has diabetes because the condition causes changes to the eyes.

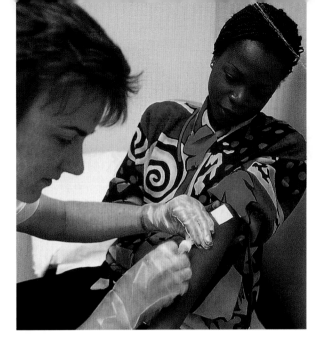

Symptoms of diabetes

- A strong thirst and a dry mouth.
- Endless trips to the toilet.
- Lack of energy and tiredness.
- Blurred vision.
- Weight loss.

Diabetes is easily diagnosed with a simple blood test.

Type 2 diabetes

Type 2 diabetes usually affects people over 40. The pancreas makes some insulin, but not enough for the body's needs. People with type 2 may be overweight or eating the wrong sort of food. The condition develops slowly and the symptoms are usually less severe than in type 1. People with type 2 do not usually need to inject insulin. They take tablets to make the pancreas work harder and may need to change to a healthier diet.

Diagnosing diabetes

Diabetes is diagnosed by testing the sugar levels in blood and urine samples. Diabetes is confirmed if the levels are very high. People with type 1 diabetes may be diagnosed in hospital and are cared for at a hospital clinic. People with type 2 are usually treated by their doctor.

Type 2 diabetes usually develops later in life.

Did you know?

- People with undiagnosed diabetes are incredibly thirsty. Young children have been found drinking from toilets and ponds.
- In the past, doctors diagnosed diabetes by tasting a person's urine to see if it was sweet!

9

Injecting insulin

Young people with diabetes need to have regular injections of insulin. Giving yourself injections or giving them to children sounds scary. But diabetes has to be treated this way.

Giving an injection

Giving injections is something most people would find a challenge. But people with diabetes cannot take insulin in a tablet because it is destroyed by juices in the stomach.

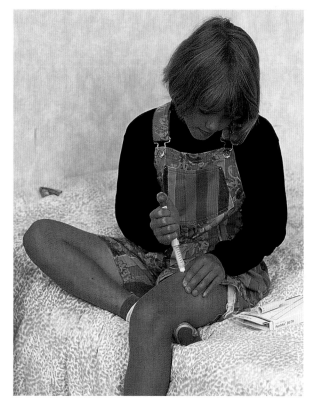

Injecting can be tricky at first, but like many things it comes with practice.

Most people inject themselves two to four times a day with a tool called an insulin pen. Some people use a **syringe**.

Where to inject?

The best places to inject are in the fatty parts of the body. It is important to change injection sites regularly or the skin may become lumpy and sore.

Where to inject insulin

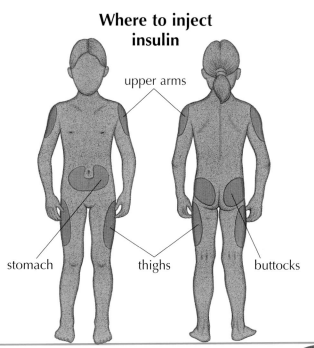

upper arms

stomach   thighs   buttocks

All about insulin

People who are just starting to use insulin are given a recommended starting **dose**. As they become more experienced they can use more or less insulin, according to their blood sugar level (see pages 14-15). Supplies of insulin last for two to three years if they are stored in the fridge. Injecting cold insulin is painful, though, so it should be brought up to room temperature first.

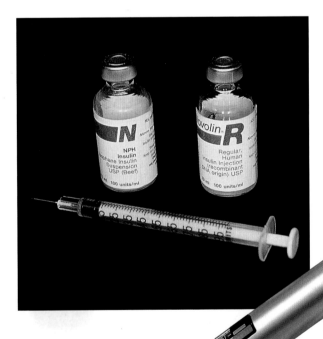

People with diabetes soon become used to handling a syringe (above) or an insulin pen (right).

How to inject with an insulin pen

1 Wash your hands and make sure that the injection site is clean.
2 Dial up the units for your insulin dose.
3 Pinch a fold of skin between your thumb and finger and push the needle into the skin.
4 Put your thumb on top of the plunger and inject all the insulin.
5 Count to five. Take the needle out slowly, keeping it straight.

'I did my first injection in hospital, two days after I was diagnosed. The nurse showed me what to do and I practised on an orange to begin with. In the end, I just stuck the needle in. Five minutes later I was in tears. Not because it hurt particularly, but because it had dawned on me that I'd be doing injections for the rest of my life.'

KATY LOUISE, AGE 17

Who gets diabetes?

Diabetes can affect anyone from newborn babies to the very old. Coping with it can be a challenge at any age.

The causes of diabetes

Doctors do not know why some people get diabetes and others do not, but there are several possible reasons. Diabetes seems to run in families, although it is hard to predict who will develop it. In some people, the condition is caused by damage to the pancreas after an infection or illness. Diet and stress may also play a part.

Did you know?

- Every year 60 000 people in the UK are diagnosed with diabetes.
- Diabetes is not an infection. You cannot catch it from somebody else, nor can you pass it on.
- Diabetes is not caused by eating sweets or the wrong foods.
- Smoking is very harmful if you have diabetes. It increases the risk of problems in later life.

Young children

Diabetes in very young children has to be managed by their parents. They need to learn to give injections, take blood tests (see pages 14-15) and think carefully about their children's eating habits. Many parents are anxious if their child is a fussy eater and worry about hurting them with an injection.

Several members of the same family may have diabetes.

Foot care

Diabetes can narrow the **blood vessels** so that less blood reaches the feet. Even small infections can be very slow to heal, so it's important to look after your feet.

1 Check your feet daily for cuts or blisters.
2 Wash your feet daily and dry them well. Rub cream into the skin if it is dry.
3 Keep your feet warm.
4 Always wear well-fitting shoes.

People with diabetes often have cold feet. Wearing thick socks or slippers helps keep the feet warm.

Teenagers

Most teenagers can manage their diabetes and handle the injections. But keeping control of the condition means thinking ahead and sticking to regular mealtimes, which becomes more difficult in the teenage years.

Older people

People are much more likely to have diabetes when they are older. They usually have type 2. This means they rarely have to manage injections, but may have to make big changes to their lifestyle – such as giving up smoking, doing more exercise and eating a healthier diet.

Health problems

High blood sugar levels can harm the body over many years. If people don't control their diabetes, they have more chance of developing health problems in the future. These include **heart attacks**, eye damage and kidney damage, and foot and leg problems.

As children grow older, they find it harder to stick to regular mealtimes.

Checking sugar levels

The amount of sugar in our blood changes during the day. If you have diabetes it is important to be aware of these changes.

To test the level of sugar in blood, first prick the side of a fingertip. Then put a drop of blood on to a blood-testing strip.

Up and down

When we eat or drink, our blood sugar level rises. Later, as glucose enters our cells, the level falls. If we exercise, it falls much faster. For most of us, the pancreas works in step with our blood sugar. When the level is high, it makes enough insulin to bring it down to normal; when it is low, the pancreas makes less insulin so that it doesn't drop any further.

Keeping a balance

People with diabetes have to control their blood sugar levels themselves. This means thinking about the food they eat, the amount of insulin they inject and the amount of exercise they do. All three things must be kept in balance. The only way to do this is by checking the sugar in their blood – in other words, by doing four or five blood tests every day. Blood-testing strips and electronic meters make testing easier.

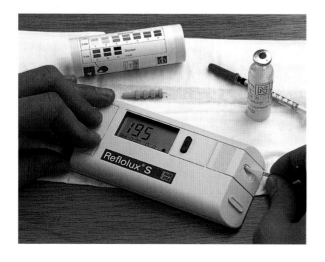

Put the blood-testing strip into an electronic meter to give an instant sugar level reading.

Good times to do a blood test

- Before each main meal.
- Before and after exercise.
- Two hours after a meal.
- Before bedtime.
- At night if you are worried about blood sugar levels dropping too low while you sleep.

Always do extra tests if you feel tired or unwell, if you travel abroad, or if your daily routine changes.

Recording results

It is important to record blood test results, either in a diary or a meter's electronic memory. At the clinic, the doctor and diabetes nurse use the results to check that blood sugar levels are being kept within safe limits. Over a period of time, they can see whether the insulin dose is right or needs changing. For example, a teenager who suddenly starts to grow probably needs a larger dose.

Did you know?

- Fingertips are good places for blood testing because the blood vessels lie near the surface.
- There are fewer nerve endings on the sides of the fingertips. This makes testing less painful.
- Scientists are working on a painless blood test that uses a laser beam.
- People who control their blood sugar well are more likely to avoid future health problems.

Putting the hands in warm water before doing a blood test helps the blood to flow more easily.

Highs and lows

People with diabetes find that controlling blood sugar levels is not always easy. Sometimes the sugar level is too low and sometimes it is too high. This may make them feel unwell.

The highs

Having high blood sugar is known as **hyperglycaemia**. The symptoms of this are the same as when a person is first diagnosed with diabetes. They are thirsty, keep going to the toilet, feel tired and start to lose weight. Hyperglycaemia may be caused by infections, by eating too many sugary foods, by not taking enough insulin or by missing injections. It is important to correct high blood sugar, as it can lead to health problems in later life.

Feeling strange and slightly dizzy are often the first warning signs of a hypo.

The lows

Having low blood sugar is known as **hypoglycaemia** (or hypo for short). Someone may have a hypo for several reasons – if they eat later than usual, have an unexpected burst of exercise or inject too much insulin, for example. A hypo comes on quite quickly and there are many warning signs. The person may look pale, feel dizzy, have a headache or start to sweat.

A child who is feeling too tired to play may have hyperglycaemia.

A hypo can be treated quickly by drinking fruit juice, and then eating something sweet.

Sometimes a person who has a hypo may lose their temper suddenly or find it hard to concentrate. Most people with diabetes recognize these signs and take steps to raise their blood sugar. But if they don't, then someone else has to do it for them – immediately. If a hypo is not treated, the person may become **unconscious**.

How to treat a hypo

1 Give a fast-acting carbohydrate drink, such as fruit juice, and then a few sweets, glucose tablets or a mini-chocolate bar.
2 When the person starts to feel better, give them a starchy snack, such as a sandwich or some biscuits and milk.
3 If the person is unconscious, do not try to feed them. Lie them on their side with their chin tilted up. If they don't recover after a few minutes, call an ambulance.

Avoiding hypos

Always carrying a few sweets or glucose tablets is a simple way to help avoid hypos. Many people with diabetes carry an identity card or bracelet so that they get the right treatment if they become unconscious. After a hypo, it's important to do a blood test to make sure the blood sugar level is back to normal.

A starchy snack such as a sandwich steadies the body's sugar level after a hypo.

The diabetes clinic

Everyone with diabetes visits a diabetes clinic regularly. Here, a team of nurses, doctors and **dieticians** check that the diabetes is under control and give advice and support.

At the clinic

People with diabetes are given a thorough check-up at the clinic. Over several visits a nurse weighs and measures them, looks at their blood-test results, examines their injection sites, checks their injection technique, takes a blood test and makes sure they can manage their diabetes.

The youngest people with diabetes attend a children's clinic.

Weighing and measuring give a picture of a child's general health.

There are different clinics for children, teenagers and adults. At first, children with diabetes go with a parent, but as they grow older they start to go on their own. At clinics for teenagers and adults, the staff check for other health problems, too. They take urine tests to check the kidneys, and examine feet and eyes.

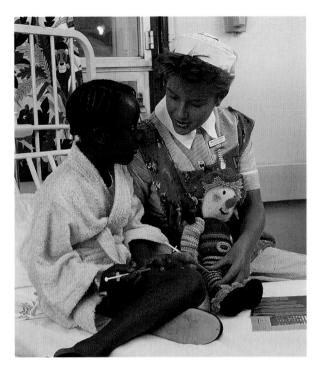

A diabetes nurse visits children with diabetes who have to stay in hospital.

Who works at a clinic?

- **Consultant** – a doctor who is an expert in diabetes. He or she is in overall charge of treatment.
- Diabetes nurse – a specially-trained nurse who gives day-to-day advice and support on how to manage diabetes.
- Dietician – a **nutrition** specialist who advises people about their diet (see pages 20-21).

Diabetes nurses

A diabetes nurse usually holds a clinic once a fortnight. Between clinics, she visits parents, schools, and anyone who needs to know more about diabetes. Her job is to educate people about the condition, explain how to deal with a hypo, and help them solve any problems. In between visits she takes phone calls from parents, answers their questions and acts as a link between families and schools, doctors and hospitals. She also visits any children with diabetes who are in hospital.

'It's pretty cool having people fussing over you when you're nervous and scared. It might seem like everyone's prodding and poking you, but after all they do know best. After a while it becomes a way of life.'

ECHO, AGE 15

A dietician advises people with diabetes about choosing a healthy diet.

Food and drink

For people with diabetes, a healthy diet is especially important to control their condition. They need to eat the right kinds of food, not only at mealtimes but in between, too.

Little and often

People with diabetes need to eat the same healthy diet recommended to everyone – low in fat, sugar and salt, high in **fibre** and with plenty of fruit and vegetables.

Fresh fruit and vegetables are an important food for everyone, especially for people with diabetes.

It is important for them to eat regularly during the day – this helps to keep blood sugar levels stable. They may need to eat snacks between mealtimes and before they go to bed.

Important foods

Carbohydrates are important for people with diabetes because these are the foods that put sugar into the blood. Starchy carbohydrates, such as potatoes, rice, bread, chapatis, pasta and cereal, release sugar slowly. They should be eaten at every meal.

A milky drink before bedtime helps to stop sugar levels dropping too low in the night.

Read the label to find out how much sugar and fat a food contains.

Dieticians

Soon after a person is diagnosed with diabetes, they will have an appointment with the dietician. Dieticians are experts on food and how it affects the body. They provide a basic plan for a healthy diet and offer plenty of advice.

Sugary carbohydrates, such as cakes, jam, ice-cream, sweets, puddings, fizzy drinks and squash, all release sugar quickly. They can send sugar levels soaring, which is why they are good for treating hypos. But as a daily food, they need to be eaten more sparingly – before exercise perhaps, or as a treat after a meal.

A slow-acting starchy carbohydrate, such as bread, should be eaten at every meal.

Healthy snacks

People with diabetes need to eat snacks between meals. Snacks can add extra fat to the diet, so it is a good idea to eat low-fat foods – fresh or dried fruit, toast, yogurt, rice cakes, breadsticks, a cereal bar or a bowl of cereal and milk.

Did you know?

- Today's low-sugar, low-fat foods are a good choice for people with diabetes.
- People with diabetes should never skip a meal. This could lead to a hypo.
- It's a good idea to avoid fizzy drinks or replace them with 'low-sugar' or 'diet' substitutes.
- Foods with the label 'diabetic' are unnecessary and are no better than ordinary foods.

Sport and exercise

Exercise is important for everyone. It's fun and it keeps you fit. Thousands of people with diabetes enjoy sports, and a very few reach the top!

Using energy

When we exercise, we burn energy, which uses up the glucose in our blood. This can cause problems for people with diabetes. If they use up too much glucose, they risk having a hypo. They can avoid this with some simple precautions.

Every activity we do burns energy.

A juicy orange boosts sugar levels half way through a match.

Before exercise

People with diabetes need extra glucose before starting any **vigorous** activity. They need to eat a snack such as a mini-chocolate bar, a cereal bar or a couple of biscuits. If the activity is likely to be long and hard, then they will need to eat even more.

During an activity

During exercise, blood sugar levels start to drop, and a person with diabetes may need some instant sugar. It is important to have some glucose tablets or a sugary drink nearby to give an extra energy boost.

Reaching the top

Steve Redgrave, world-class rower and gold medallist in five Olympics, was diagnosed with type 2 diabetes in 1998. Every day he takes five or six injections of fast-acting insulin to cope with his intense training. He eats snacks between training sessions and takes glucose tablets or a drink whenever he feels he needs a boost. He does six or seven daily blood tests to check his blood sugar levels.

'It's an advantage being a sportsman. You have to be very disciplined about your whole lifestyle. Diabetes is just another part of the equation. It's not difficult – it's a pain in the neck, but that's all really.'

STEVE REDGRAVE

People with diabetes need extra sugar during exercise, just as marathon runners do.

After exercise

Most hypos happen after exercise, so it is a good idea for people with diabetes to eat a snack and test their blood sugar level when they finish.

Did you know?

- Footballers who have diabetes often take a glucose drink before a match, and at half-time.
- People with diabetes should always carry something like a banana or cereal bar around with them in case they do any unplanned exercise.
- A person with diabetes should always tell a coach or lifeguard about their condition.

Diabetes at home

Diabetes affects the whole family. When a child is first diagnosed with the condition, injections, blood tests and planning a diet can take hours. Sometimes brothers and sisters can feel left out.

Feeling jealous

A child who has just been diagnosed with diabetes becomes the centre of attention. Life revolves around blood tests, injections and the food they eat. Other children in the family may not envy the injections, but they can still feel jealous of the attention.

It's easy for a child to feel left out when their brother or sister has diabetes.

On the other hand, children with diabetes may be upset that they have to cope with the condition when their brothers and sisters don't. It's important for the family to talk through these problems now and then. This can help to clear the air.

'Sometimes I get really upset when I see my brother and sister eating sweets whenever they want, because I feel I'm missing out.'

LOUISA, AGE 13

When a child is first diagnosed with diabetes, injections can be difficult and take a long time.

Exercise is good for people with diabetes, and for the rest of the family, too.

Support groups

Parents of children with diabetes often join support groups. Here they talk to other people who are dealing with diabetes. This helps them to feel less isolated and more confident that they can cope.

Being positive

Diabetes isn't all bad. It can have a positive effect on family life – in encouraging everybody to eat a healthier diet and to exercise more often, for example. The first months after diagnosis can be difficult, but a family soon learns to cope, and in time treats diabetes as nothing special.

Did you know?

- Brothers and sisters soon learn how to spot and treat a hypo.
- Teenagers with diabetes often refuse to do blood tests as a way of rebelling against the condition.
- In families where someone has diabetes, sweets and chocolates often cause arguments. Children with diabetes can't always eat them as often as they would like.

When someone has diabetes, it can lead to healthier mealtimes for the whole family.

Diabetes at school

Anyone who looks after children needs to understand about diabetes. This is very important at school, where all children want to feel one of the crowd and just live a normal life.

Talking to teachers

When a child is diagnosed with diabetes, or when a child with diabetes joins a school, their parents and diabetes nurse should meet the head and class teacher. They need to discuss the risk of hypos, the need for regular snacks, how to prepare for PE, and so on.

All children with diabetes need a healthy meal in the middle of the day.

School action

Schools need to fill out a record card – with contact numbers and details of how to treat a hypo – for every child with diabetes. They must inform every member of staff, too. Children who do their own injections need a private place, as well as a supply of fast-acting carbohydrates available at all times. Teachers need to tell other pupils about diabetes, and explain the need for snacks.

Children with diabetes can enjoy PE so long as they eat a snack first.

Children with diabetes can enjoy school trips, which are an important part of school life.

Holiday fun

Children with diabetes can go on specially-run holidays where they try out new activities – abseiling, canoeing, sailing and windsurfing, for example. This gives them the chance to have a break from home, make new friends and share common experiences. It makes them realize they're not the only ones with diabetes and can help them to become more confident.

Activity holidays are a good way for children with diabetes to make new friends.

School trips

Children with diabetes do not need special attention. They take part fully in school activities, including sport and PE. School trips need a little extra planning. A teacher should always carry a spare injection kit and take extra food in case of delays. Children who give themselves injections can go on overnight trips.

'I was really dreading going back to school after my diagnosis. I knew that all my friends and teachers would be fussing over me, and I was right. It was "Should you be eating that?" or "Are you feeling OK?" It drove me mad.'
TOM, AGE 13

Questions people ask

Can I drive if I have diabetes?
Yes, but you will need a special licence that has to be renewed more often than an ordinary driving licence.

Will there ever be a cure for diabetes?
Maybe. Scientists are looking at ways to **transplant** healthy insulin-producing cells from one person to another. Or they may be able to make artificial ones.

Diabetes does not prevent people from driving a car.

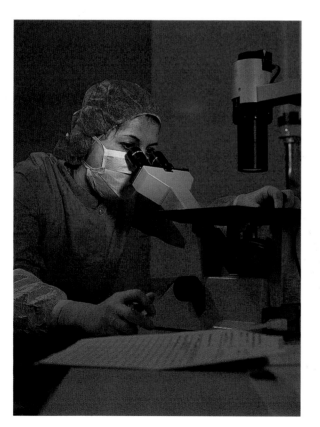

Are there any jobs I won't be able to do?
If you take insulin for diabetes, there are some jobs you won't be able to do. These include working for the police, fire service or armed forces, being a pilot, working at sea, and driving trucks, trains, buses or taxis.

Scientists are doing a great deal of research into diabetes. One day they may find a cure.

Some children inject themselves, but others like the help of a parent.

How old do you have to be to give yourself injections?
There is no right or wrong age. Some children, usually aged about ten and over, prefer to give themselves injections. Others prefer a parent to give them the injection.

Can I continue with my favourite sport now that I've got diabetes?
Definitely – Olympic rower Steve Redgrave does, and so can everyone else. But you can't box, learn to fly or go parachuting. If you plan to ski, go climbing or swim in the sea, it's wise to do this with a friend.

People with diabetes should always swim with a friend, in case they have a hypo.

Can diabetes make people blind?
People who have diabetes sometimes have problems with their eyes. Usually eye damage can be prevented by checking blood sugar levels every day and keeping them as normal as possible. Annual eye check-ups are important so that any problems can be treated early.

Glossary

bloodstream The flow of blood around the body.

blood vessel A tube that carries blood around the body.

carbohydrate An important source of energy that is found in starchy or sugary foods such as potatoes, rice, bread, pasta, sweets and biscuits.

cell One of the billions of tiny building blocks that make up a plant or animal.

chapati An Indian bread that is flat.

consultant A doctor who is trained to treat a particular condition or who works in a particular area of medicine.

diagnose To discover what type of illness a person has.

dietician Someone who is an expert on food and how it affects the body.

dose The amount of medicine given to a patient.

fibre A bulky material that our bodies can't digest. It is found in foods like brown rice, wholemeal bread and vegetables. Fibre helps keep the digestive system healthy.

gland An organ that produces substances which are used for certain jobs inside the body, such as digesting food.

glucose A type of sugar in the food we eat and which we use as fuel.

heart attack A blockage in one of the arteries, or tubes, which supply blood to the heart. Without blood, parts of the heart muscle may stop pumping and die.

hyperglycaemia A higher than normal amount of sugar in the blood. Someone with hyperglycaemia feels thirsty and has to keep going to the toilet. They also feel tired and begin to lose weight.

hypoglycaemia (also called a **hypo**) A lower than normal amount of sugar in the blood. Someone having a hypo may look pale, feel dizzy, have a headache or start to sweat. They may also lose their temper suddenly or find it hard to concentrate.

insulin A chemical made by a gland called the pancreas. It controls the level of sugar in the blood.

kidney One of the two organs that take waste substances from the blood and turn them into urine.

nutrition The study of foods needed by the body to work properly.

pancreas A gland near the stomach that produces insulin, as well as juices to digest food.

plantain A tropical fruit like a large banana with a green skin.

starchy Containing a lot of starch – a white, powdery carbohydrate that has no taste or smell. Starchy foods include bread, chapati, plantain, potatoes, pasta, cereals and rice.

symptom One of the signs of a disease. A strong thirst is a symptom of diabetes, for example.

syringe A tool that is used to take samples of blood and to inject substances into the body.

transplant To remove an organ from an animal or a person and replace it with another.

unconscious Asleep or unaware.

urine The yellow waste liquid that leaves our bodies when we go to the toilet.

vigorous Energetic.

Further information

To find out more about diabetes, contact:

Diabetes UK
10 Queen Anne Street
London W1G 9LH

Tel: 020 7636 6112 (careline)
e-mail: careline@diabetes.org.uk
Website: www.diabetes.org.uk

Index

blood sugar level 6-7, 9, 11, 13, 14-17, 20, 22, 23, 29

blood tests 5, 9, 12, 14, 15, 17, 18, 23, 24, 25

cakes and biscuits 7, 17, 21, 22

carbohydrates 6, 7, 17, 20, 21, 26, 30

causes of diabetes 12

cells 6, 7, 14, 28, 30

clinic 9, 15, 18-19

consultant 19, 30

cure for diabetes 8, 28

diagnosing diabetes 8, 9, 30

diet 8, 9, 12, 13, 19, 20-21, 24, 25

dietician 18-19, 21, 30

doctors 8, 9, 12, 15, 18-19

drinking 7, 14, 17, 20-21, 22, 23

driving 28

exercise 8, 13, 14, 15, 16, 21, 22-23, 25

eyes 5, 8, 13, 18, 29

families 12, 24-24

feet 5, 13, 18

fibre 20, 30

food and eating 4, 5, 6, 7, 8, 9, 12, 13, 14, 16, 17, 20-21, 24, 25, 26, 27

fruit and vegetables 20, 21, 22, 23

fruit juice 17

glucose 6, 7, 14, 17, 22, 23, 30

heart attacks 13, 30

home life 24-25

hospital 9, 11, 19

hyperglycaemia 16, 30

hypoglycaemia 16-17, 19, 21, 22, 23, 25, 26, 29, 31

identity cards 17

infections 12, 13, 16

injections 4, 5, 7, 8, 9, 10-11, 12, 13, 14, 16, 18, 23, 24, 26, 27, 29

insulin 4, 6-11, 14, 15, 16, 23, 28, 31

insulin pen 10, 11

jobs 28

kidneys 5, 6, 13, 18, 31

nurses 11, 15, 18-19, 26

older people 5, 8, 9, 12, 13, 19

pancreas 6, 7, 8, 9, 12, 14, 31

Redgrave, Steve 23, 29

schools 19, 26-27

snacks 5, 17, 20, 21, 22, 23, 26

sport 22-23, 29

starch 7, 17, 20, 21, 31

stomach 6, 10

sugar 4, 6, 7, 9, 11, 13, 14-17, 20, 21, 22, 23, 29

support groups 25

sweets 12, 17, 24, 25

swimming 29

symptoms 4, 5, 8, 9, 16, 31

syringe 10, 11, 31

thirst 8, 9, 16

tiredness 5, 7, 9, 15, 16

treatment 4, 5, 8, 9, 10-11, 17, 19, 20-21

type 1 diabetes 8, 9

type 2 diabetes 9, 13, 23

urine 7, 9, 18, 31

weight loss 5, 7, 9, 16

ACC. No: 02790470

GRANGETOWN LIBRARY
029 2023 8325

Tennis
Clive Gifford

KNOW YOUR SPORT

First published in 2007 by
Franklin Watts
338 Euston Road
London NW1 3BH

Franklin Watts Australia
Level 17/207 Kent Street
Sydney NSW 2000

© Franklin Watts 2007

Series editor: Jeremy Smith
Art director: Jonathan Hair

**Series designed and created for
Franklin Watts by Painted Fish Ltd.**
Designer: Rita Storey
Editor: Nicola Edwards
Photography: Tudor Photography,
Banbury

A CIP catalogue record
for this book is available
from the British Library.

Dewey classification:
ISBN: 978 0 7496 7406 9

Printed in China

Note: At the time of going to press, the statistics and player profiles in this book were up to date. However, due to some players' active participation in the sport, it is possible that some of these may now be out of date.

Picture credits
Glyn Kirk/Actionplus p.6; Leo Mason/Action Plus, GlynKirk/Actionplus p.9; Glyn Kirk/Actionplus p.17; Glyn Kirk/Actionplus p.19; Neil Tingle/Action Plus p.23; Richard Francis/Action Plus p.27

Cover images: Tudor Photography, Banbury.

All photos posed by models.
Thanks to Adam Akinyemi, Yan Cai, Joseph Cooper, Elizabeth Puender and Kismet Zafar

The Publisher would like to thank Bloxham School for the use of their sport facilities and Coach, Pam Eagles, for her assistance.

Taking part in sport is a fun way to get fit, but like any form of physical exercise it has an element of risk, particularly if you are unfit, overweight or suffer from any medical conditions. It is advisable to consult a healthcare professional before beginning any programme of exercise.